I AM.....SUCCESS

*A Roadmap for Defining and Fulfilling
A Life Vision of Holistic Success*

I AM.....SUCCESS

A Roadmap for Defining and Fulfilling
A Life Vision of Holistic Success

Anthony Dwane Parnell

I AM...SUCCESS
A Roadmap for Defining and Fulfilling
a Life Vision of Holistic Success

Copyright © 2018, 2016 Anthony Dwane Parnell

All rights reserved. No part of this publication may be reproduced, distributed, or transmitted in any form or by any means, including photocopying, recording, or other electronic or mechanical methods, without the prior written permission of the publisher, except in the case of brief quotations embodied in critical reviews and certain other noncommercial uses permitted by copyright law.

Books by Anthony Parnell
Las Vegas, Nevada

ISBN# 978-0-9644205-5-7
Library of Congress Control Number: 2018908980

Cover design and Images by Roel Sanchez
Editing by Paul Morehouse, PhD

www.BooksbyAnthonyParnell.com

www.AnthonyParnell.com

TABLE OF CONTENTS

CHAPTER 1
Embrace the Philosophy:
There is No One Path to Success 1

CHAPTER 2
Embrace a Holistic Definition and
Approach to Success 11

CHAPTER 3
Develop and Implement
an Efficient Plan of Action 33

CHAPTER 4
Trust in Your Power to Manifest Your Life Vision
(Trust in the Manifestation) 57

CHAPTER 5
Fulfill Your Vision of Success
(Your Life Vision) 77

TABLE OF CONTENTS (Cont'd.)

POEMS
"The Ultimate Life Goal".. 31/101
"The Words of a Philosopher"................................ 34
"I AM…SUCCESS"... 75
"A Mantra of Success".. 78
"Forgive Yourself for Past Failures......................... 89

TABLES and CHARTS
Seven Core Areas of Life Balance........................... 14
Self-Care Monitoring Chart..................................... 18-19
Orman's 5 Laws of Money....................................... 22
Environmental Concerns: Things You Can Do to Help… 25
Sources (for Environmental Concerns)................... 26
Barriers to Achieving Your Goals............................ 83-85

WORKSHEETS and EXERCISES
Life Purpose Questions 30
Life Balance Report Card.. 39
Primary Goals 42-48
Prioritizing Your Goals.. 49-52
Sample Step-by-Step Goals 54
Visual Imagery Exercise 72-73
Strategies (for Barriers) 86-88
Greatest Disappointments..................................... 91
5 Minutes A Day Of Writing................................... 94
6 Steps To Picking Up the Pen............................... 95-97

Embrace the Philosophy: There is No One Path to Success

"There is no one path to success.

I repeat….
there is no one path to success."

A Path to Understanding Holistic Success

My experience as a young adult was both beautiful and challenging. On the one hand, I was fervently engaged in self-reflection and self-exploration, determined to find the secret to intrapersonal healing and inner peace. Essentially, I was consumed with and committed to discovering and developing the "inner" person. I attended numerous seminars and lectures, reading countless books on self-help, self-improvement, cultural identity and spirituality. Like most young adults, I was deeply concerned about the direction my life would take. It was very clear to me that I did not want to choose a career just because it guaranteed a high-level income. My deepest aspirations were for a more *holistic success*, that is, fulfilment as a whole human being – achieving balance in mind, body and spirit!

Admittedly, I did not escape being drawn into a wealth consciousness. At one point, my strategy was, literally, to have lots of money. So, for years, I tried again and again to find my path to success. But, my heart kept reminding me: holistic success is not just about the *end game*; holistic success does not turn a blind eye to the path that one takes to achieve the desired goal; that the *means* is just as important as the *end*!

There was a time when I wanted to be a musician; then a college professor; then a social worker; then an author. In other words, I had no problem with identifying goals. What always seemed to evade me was a sense of my path; the course of action that I needed to follow to reach a particular goal. I just didn't know how to keep moving toward the goal while simultaneously pursuing, developing, and discovering my true, highest Self.

A Lesson is Learned

What I learned after years of anguish and frustration is that there is no one path to success. Instead, there is a combination of variables that differ from person-to-person. These variables are distinct and relative to the life history of the individual and the particular goal that they are pursuing.

Some argue that the primary determining factor to achieving success is *hard work* and *fierce determination*.

Others argue that it is *faith* – that is, having a strong belief system.

While hard work, fierce determination and faith can be critical elements in the pursuit of most goals, I don't agree that they are the sole determining factors as to whether or not an individual achieves long-term success or even one particular life goal. Instead, I believe that the variables for achieving success differ significantly from person to person and from one situation to another.

What about a child who is born into a wealthy family? Of no fault of their own, there are no financial limitations when considering what career or occupation to pursue. Hard work definitely will pay off, but we can't say it's the dominant factor in determining their success. In addition to economic factors, there is a clear advantage for children who are exposed to a "success mindset" from an early age. By growing up with financial comfort, seeds were planted early in life–consciously or subconsciously–that the world is filled with unlimited potential for them and that money should never be perceived as an obstacle to pursuing their dreams and passions. So, when considering their successes, how much can we attribute to their own efforts and how much to the environment they were born into?

It is my belief that individuals can be programmed for success just as they can be programmed for failure.

What about the child who grows up without a great support system of loving, healthy, and grounded parents who never miss a baseball game or an award ceremony? While it's true a great home life doesn't guarantee that a child will reach their full potential or even do something positive with their life, when a child is not raised in a loving, healthy, grounded home they typically have a much harder road to navigate in life. There are many more psychological hurdles with which they must contend. Even if they complete their education and find a good career, they still are likely to have a significant amount of emotional residue that they must try to resolve as an adult. This is an arduous process that can take many years.

Is this person going to measure their success predominantly by how much money they have in the bank, or by the position they hold at their job, or by how many square feet their house measures?

The point I'm trying to make is that a big part of success is what it means to you as an individual. Where did you start in life? Where are you now? And, are you still making forward progress or are you stuck?

Once again, there is no one path to success, just as there is no "one size fits all" definition of success. While there may be fundamental elements to achieving success, the picture of how success is painted in a person's life is something that is original and unique to them. In other words, success is not the same for everyone. Success can be measured in a variety of ways.

Of course, one aspect of success will be measured by what you materialize, manifest, and create in the world. But, the other part of success is something that cannot be found in the physical and material world outside of yourself. It can only be found on the inside—through inner growth and self-awareness. Ultimately, to achieve success both internally and externally, you must figure out the right combination of variables that will put you on a path to not just professional success but *holistic* success in life.

We, as a society, tend to place greater emphasis on one form of success over another, i.e., financial success is more important than being successful as a spouse, as a parent or as a kind and loving person who treats others with respect. And, as a result, many individuals succumb to societal pressure by allowing themselves to be identified with socially-generated superficial definitions of success when it generally has nothing to do with what is truly most important and valuable in life.

Whether you're 50 years old or 20 years old, what it means to be successful is something that most individuals will wrestle with at some point in their lives and maybe for the duration of their lives. There will always be pressure to live up to the expectations of others and the definitions of success promoted by society. However, it's up to you to break through the false social conventions and to hold on to something that is much more substantive and fulfilling for who YOU are as a unique individual!

For this breakthrough to occur, there must be a shift in your belief system.

You must adopt a broader definition of success.

Well, believe me. I know that this is much easier said than done.

To begin with, it is hard to find role models - individuals who truly experience holistic success. These are people who are in a profession they love, generate the income they desire, nurture whole and healthy relationships, and are generally in tune with what they believe to be their life purpose. The scarcity of such people makes it difficult for most of us to conceptualize holistic success for ourselves. Most of us believe that aspects of ourselves and our aspirations must be sacrificed in this pursuit. We are prisoners to the belief that we can't be financially well-off while still being a grounded, loving, whole, and healthy person; that we can't make a comfortable living following our true passion and doing what we love; that during the years of child-rearing responsibilities, we have to forego our life-long dreams and things that are personally fulfilling to us.

To me, these are just limiting beliefs reflecting a person's social conditioning and/or their fear of failure.

"I AM…SUCCESS" is a mindset that says "I" can pursue my life goals and achieve them. And, that the barometer or measuring stick for my success is not primarily based on status, power, or financial wealth.

"I" am not just a material, physical being. "I" am a spiritual being, an emotional being, an intellectual being. All of these different aspects of me are what creates the total sum of who "I" am.

"I", therefore, no longer need to define my success by just one aspect of myself or by what "I" accomplish financially and materially. Instead, my ultimate pursuit in life will be to become the most well-rounded, complete person "I" can possibly be.

While pursuing my personal and professional goals, I'm going to commit myself to being the best father or mother, the best husband or wife, the best co-worker, the best teammate, the best citizen in my community.

I'm going to explore, identify, and fully pursue what "I" believe to be my life purpose and life calling.

I'm going to live with this belief and mindset: *Life blesses me daily and in every moment simply by having air to breathe. I will practice living in a constant state of giving and reciprocity in all that I do. As a result, my life will embody true holistic success, happiness, and fulfillment.*

This, in a nutshell, is the "I AM…SUCCESS" philosophy and what this book is about.

By reading this book and adopting the life philosophy it presents, you will no longer have to struggle to fit your goals and aspirations into a narrow definition of success that comes only from a statistical cultural perspective and not your personal journey! Here I present a definition of success that is holistic in the way it encompasses all aspects of your goals and desires financially, spiritually, physically, and in your relationships.

Within this book, I also lay out some steps you can take to begin looking at your entire life from a holistic perspective. This is in direct contrast to a one-dimensional perspective that comes from being overly consumed with pursuing and accomplishing one particular goal in just one area of your life.

In Chapter 3, I invite you to set clear goals in "Seven Core Areas" of your life and to write out clear action steps for pursuing each of your goals.

The bigger piece of the puzzle is finding those elements of your life vision that are uniquely yours. This stems from knowing yourself. If you feel you don't know yourself, it might be wise to invest some time and energy to explore some of the basic questions such as "Why am I here?" "What difference can I make in other people's lives if I use my God-given talents and abilities?" Such inquiry requires a willingness to be honest with yourself and the courage to continue to seek answers. As answers are revealed, the task then is to embrace these truths and to follow-through with implementing the newfound knowledge into your life.

I fully understand and accept that not everyone will agree with my philosophy nor have the willingness to commit to the pursuit of a holistic definition of success. It is not my place to judge those who feel the need to pursue money, power and status as the ultimate symbols of success. My mission in life is not to convert people but rather to help those who are feeling stuck: individuals who simply feel they need a jumpstart in order to make real progress in the pursuit of their goals; people looking for the key that will open new doors to success – not in just one area but in *all* areas of their life.

If my holistic approach to success resonates with you, I am super excited for you and would love to hear from you! Please let me know how this book has helped you and what specific actions you have taken since reading it.

Visit my website at **www.AnthonyParnell.com** or email me at **anthony@anthonyparnell.com**.

Thanks to everyone who reads this book!

Anthony Parnell, M.S.W.

I AM...SUCCESS

Chapter 2

Embrace a Holistic Definition and Approach to Success

"Holistic success is not defined simply by how much money you make.

It's also defined by the difference you make."

Anthony Parnell

Success is not defined simply by reaching a final destination. Success is not solely an event for which we are waiting to happen. Success is our promise to shape ourselves through a daily process as we proceed on our journey toward the fulfillment of our desires.

Success is a mindset, thought process, and approach to life that fuels the decisions we make and the values that we hold. Success is total commitment to being the best person we can be in each and every moment. It is putting our best foot forward and making the best decisions we can make in any given situation.

Success does not lie solely in the occupational position we hold or the material things we possess. We are much more than the money we make and the cars we drive. We are ever evolving creatures of unlimited intellectual, physical, and emotional capacity. Success, then, encompasses all aspects of who we are as human beings and the quality of our relationships with others. The word "quality" here is key. Many people have their egos stroked if they have a long list of friends. Yet, numbers (quantity) do not necessarily guarantee the quality of our relationships. I believe we can claim success in our relationships – even if the list is short - *when there is real trust and genuine caring that is reciprocal.*

Most importantly, success is not one-dimensional but rather multi-dimensional. It is giving, and it is receiving. It is what we fully embrace as our best selves at this particular moment of our lives, and it is our hopes and dreams for the future embodied in our commitment to reach our fullest potential in all areas of our lives - mentally, physically and spiritually.

SEVEN CORE AREAS OF LIFE BALANCE

The phrase "Mind, Body and Spirit" is one that is frequently associated with health and wellness and the cultivation of spirituality. In developing my philosophy of holistic success, I have added four additional areas of health and wellness that can also be viewed as life strengths. I refer to them as the Seven Core Areas of Life Balance.

The concept of Seven Core Areas of Life Balance challenges an individual to broaden his or her perception of success, health and wellness by embracing a multi-dimensional perspective. It does not focus on accomplishing just one goal or achieving success in just one area. Success and wellness, for example, are not measured solely by being physically fit or having a great career. The Seven Core Areas of Life Balance speaks to the many interrelated elements of our internal and external existence as a human being.

Thus, the Seven Core Areas of Life Balance provides a general framework for how we can view and assess health, wellness, balance, and harmony in every corner of our lives. Just as poor health and disease can exist in the physical body, disharmony and imbalances can also occur in our finances, our relationships, our mental and emotional states, and so on. By individually assessing each core area, it enables us to focus on how to strengthen and improve our health in each individual core area.

On the following pages, I provide a summary and overview of each of the Seven Core Areas of Life Balance.

SEVEN CORE AREAS OF LIFE BALANCE

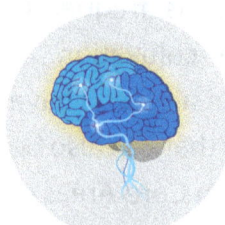

Healthy Mind

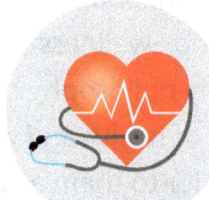

Healthy Body

Healthy Spirit

Healthy Finances

Healthy Relationships

Healthy Profession/Career

A Clear Sense of Life Purpose

CORE AREA ❶
Healthy Mind

Maintaining a healthy mental state is critical for finding balance and harmony in each of the other core areas of our life.

From my personal experience, affirmations are an excellent tool that can be utilized to aid in maintaining a healthy mind. In case you're not familiar with affirmations, here are a few examples:

I am at Peace in my Life.
Love and fulfillment surrounds me.

My body is healed.
My mind is strong.
And,
I have a clear sense of my life purpose.

~

Each of the seven core areas of my life
are in balance,
in harmony
and improving day by day.

~

I AM...SUCCESS

I feel powerful.

I am powerful.

*I am manifesting
anything and everything I want
in life.*

As a starting point, there are a number of other tools and exercises that can be utilized to help you maintain a healthy state of mind:

- Take time daily for self-reflection.
- Surround yourself with positive people, places and things.
- Maintain a mindset of gratitude.

More than anything, you should muster the willingness to seek the help of others when you are unable to restore mental balance and harmony on your own. This may even include utilizing the expertise of a mental health therapist.

> **NOTE:** The comments provided in this book should not replace the advice of licensed healthcare professionals.

 **CORE AREA 2**
Healthy Body

There are various interpretations of what constitutes physical health and many different prescribed methods for maintaining it. One doctor will emphasize preventative measures such as caloric intake and diet while another doctor will emphasize exercise and sleep. It can become rather confusing on what to focus your attention on. Here are some essential elements of health that can easily be implemented and monitored in one's daily life.

- An adequate amount of sleep
- Sufficient water intake
- Appropriate physical exercise
- Proper diet (monitoring calories, fats, sugars, and carbohydrates)
- Recreational outlets/hobby

Below is a chart that you can use to set goals and/or track some key areas of your activities related to maintaining a Healthy Body. The first mini-chart has already been completed to provide you with some examples of how you can complete your personal Self-Care Monitoring Chart.

I AM...SUCCESS

Self-Care Monitoring Chart

EXAMPLE

	ADEQUATE AMOUNT OF SLEEP	WATER INTAKE	PHYSICAL EXERCISE	DIET (Caloric, Fat, Sugar, and Carbohydrate intake)	RECREATIONAL OUTLET/ HOBBY
WEDNESDAY	6 hours	½ Gallon		2,000 Calories No Soda or Dessert	Choir Practice
THURSDAY	9 hours	1 Gallon	Jogged	2,500 Calories Only 1 Piece of Cake but too many Carbs	

Self-Care Monitoring Chart

	ADEQUATE AMOUNT OF SLEEP	WATER INTAKE	PHYSICAL EXERCISE	DIET (Caloric, Fat, Sugar, and Carbohydrate intake)	RECREATIONAL OUTLET/ HOBBY
SUNDAY					
MONDAY					
TUESDAY					
WEDNESDAY					
THURSDAY					
FRIDAY					
SATURDAY					
SUNDAY					
MONDAY					
TUESDAY					
WEDNESDAY					
THURSDAY					
FRIDAY					
SATURDAY					

NOTE: The comments provided in this book should not replace the advice of licensed healthcare professionals.

CORE AREA ③
HEALTHY SPIRIT

Spirituality can be defined as: one's belief in and connection to a higher power; the embodiment of the life sustaining and life generating principles of love, balance, harmony and shared abundance; the ability to manifest.

The essence of life is spiritual. Everything in the material world emanates from an invisible, spiritual source. Spirit represents not only our connection to all human beings but our connection to a higher power. Because of our spiritual nature, we can feel the presence of others and impact their thoughts and emotions without being in the same physical location.

I once heard a person say that our persona is actually the vibration that we emit. Or, another way of saying it is that our persona is the energy that people feel when they see, talk or interact with us. This is because when we meet and interact with others we trigger positive or negative emotions within them. While this has much to do with the person with whom we're interacting, it also is an indication of our own current mental and emotional state, both of which, in turn, influence how we are able to connect with or tune-in to our spiritual state.

The point I'm trying to make is that spirit or energy-vibrations are the essential nature of all material life. A healthy connection to spirit, then, refers to our ability to connect to the non-physical part of ourselves which encompasses our emotional state. When our connection to spirit is strong, we are vibrating one kind of energy.

And, when our connection to spirit is low or compromised, we are vibrating a different kind of energy.

CORE AREA 4
Healthy Finances

Healthy Finances represents the cultivation of a mindset of abundance. In this mindset we are always able to attract into our life all the financial and material resources needed and desired. Healthy Finances also represents responsible and effective money management. When wealth consciousness and effective money management are operating in our life, we feel a sense of personal power.

Just as the field of medicine offers a plethora of medical experts with wide ranging opinions and recommendations for achieving and maintaining physical health, the world of finance is saturated with experts on financial health as well. One of the most profound concepts I have encountered for making sound financial decisions and assessing financial health is Suze Orman's "Five Laws of Money" (Orman, 2003). Her five laws of money represent a basic philosophy of money management and financial decision-making. Even more, I have found these five laws of money to be simple, easy to understand, and applicable to individuals from all income levels.

Orman's 5 Laws of Money

Law #1: Truth Creates Money, Lies Destroy It

Law #2: Look at What You Have, Not at What You Had

Law #3: Do What is Right for You, Before You Do What Is Right for Your Money

Law #4: Invest in the Known Before the Unknown

Law #5: Always Remember: Money Has No Power of Its Own

CORE AREA 5
Healthy and Fulfilling Relationships

Healthy and Fulfilling Relationships encompasses two distinct components. One is our "Relationships with Others" and the other is our "Relationship with the Earth" (with Nature).

Relationships with Others

The accumulation of mental, emotional and physical clutter robs us of our energy and the ability to maintain balance and well-being. To our own detriment, cluttered relationships create additional roadblocks to achieving our goals. Yet, few people are willing to be completely honest or careful when examining the negative impact that certain relationships have on their personal and professional life.

What is a healthy relationship? In its simplest form, relationships are an exchange of energy. The things we say, the things we do, and the thoughts we think are all aspects of how we relate to one another.

In healthy relationships, what a person does, says, and thinks builds up the other person by sending them positive energy. This is why it's so important to (consistently) surround yourself with positive people.

Learning to set healthy boundaries with family and friends can be a very challenging and painful process. An important part of the challenge is learning how to say "No!" Many of us compete with intense feelings of guilt when faced with constant requests for our time, energy, or even money by those close to us. This is often due to the fact that many of us live by the belief that we must be willing to sacrifice anything and everything for loved ones no matter the circumstances or the consequences. Yet, without realizing it, we may be blinded by our personal beliefs and fail to realize that family and friends do not always share the same values. Consequently, we feel let down when they are not willing to make the same sacrifices and compromises that we are willing to make.

Tremendous effort is required to learn how to make distinctions between relationships that drain your energy and those that motivate and inspire you. Self-awareness and honesty, with yourself and others, are necessary ingredients. Concurrently, you must begin to accept that most individuals, over time, develop a set of expectations based on past experiences. By expanding your self-awareness and increasing your sense of personal responsibility and self-discipline, you will be better able to determine the boundaries that are necessary for healthy relationships and, once established, to consistently maintain those boundaries for the betterment of yourself and everyone in your life.

Relationship with the Earth (Nature)

Our relationship with nature, with the earth and the resources of the earth, is definitely one of critical importance. We need the resources of the earth to survive. Furthermore, given that relationships with one's self and with others happen within larger environmental contexts, it is always in our best interest to view ourselves as stewards and caretakers of the earth. Thus, as part of our pursuit of a *holistic* vision of success, we should strive to find a healthy balance in our utilization and consumption of the earth's resources and our overall impact on the environment.

There are many arguments as to which environmental concerns should be given the highest priority and how best to approach them. This is an expansive topic. So, the information that I am able to give here is limited. In the table on the following page, I have listed a number of "Environmental Concerns" as well as "Things You Personally Can Do" to improve the environment.

Embrace a Holistic Definition and Approach to Success

ENVIRONMENTAL CONCERNS	THINGS YOU CAN DO TO HELP THE ENVIRONMENT (Solutions to Environmental Concerns)
Air Pollution	Reduce, Reuse, Recycle- (EPA Recommendation) "See Below"
Water Pollution	
Global Warming	Reduce the Carbon Footprint of Your Car
Climate Change	· Drive Better · Regular Maintenance · Proper Tire Inflation
Overpopulation	· Make your next vehicle a fuel-efficient one
Natural Resource Depletion	· Household fuel efficiency (usage of more than one car in a home)
Waste Disposal	Unplug all unnecessary appliances
Loss of Biodiversity	Adjust your thermostat
Deforestation	Turn off your lights
Ocean Acidification	Use energy efficient light bulbs
Ozone Layer Depletion	Compost your grass clippings and organic waste Buy products with reduced packaging
Acid Rain	Ride a bike or walk to work or shopping
Urban Sprawl	Carpool or use public transportation
Public Health Issues	Sparingly use insecticides, herbicides and fertilizers, as well as other lawn and garden chemicals, and always follow label directions
Genetic Engineering	

SOURCES

EPA (US Environmental Protection Agency)

www.epa.gov/recycle

www3.epa.gov/climatechange/wycd/

U.S. Department of Energy

www.Energy.gov

Other Sources

http://www.empoweringretreat.com/green-tips.html

www.footprintnetwork.org

https://carbonfund.org/reduce/

http://wwf.panda.org/how_you_can_help/live_green/

http://www.miwaterstewardship.org/residents/learnaboutourwater/watermanagementbestpractices/listofpositiveenvironmentalpractices

CORE AREA 6
Healthy and Fulfilling Profession/Career

People who really enjoy what they do for a living are blessed! Many individuals are employed in positions that only serve the primary function of enabling them to provide for themselves and their family. It's icing on the cake when an individual is able to earn a good living in a job or profession that is also personally fulfilling.

Some people are fortunate to know early in life what profession will bring them fulfilment. For others, it requires many years of exploration and intense soul searching.

When we don't have a clear idea of the kind of career or profession that will fulfill us, we must be willing to explore our passions, gifts, and abilities – always ready to go deeper and learn more about ourselves. Then, we, must have the courage to pursue the career path that we begin to envision for ourselves.

Unfortunately, the fear of venturing into the unknown holds many of us back from pursuing our "dream job." If we have limited role models and don't know people who are fulfilled in their career or profession of choice, it can be much harder for us to believe in our own ability to achieve the career goal we desire. To minimize anxiety, it can be helpful to create a plan for exploring alternative professions – careers either directly related to our "first choice" or maybe some that are very different. Strategies to consider as part of a plan of exploration might include one or more of the following: 1) Take a career profile exam. 2) Read books about the professions that interest you. 3) Take some entry level courses in a field that attracts you to see if your level of interest remains strong or wanes.

There is a saying, "Where you are tomorrow is dictated by what you do today." Therefore, thinking ahead to the future and not allowing yourself to wallow in regrets about the past should provide some degree of motivation to start moving in the right direction. If you can, see yourself waking up each day and looking forward to going to work. The desire to pursue something more fulfilling is alive within you; you just have to be willing to steadily move towards it.

It is possible that a major sacrifice and complete career change may not be necessary. You may just need to make a slight shift or adjustment in your current job duties by transferring to a new department or relocating to another city or another company in the same field. The truth of the matter is that there are endless opportunities and possibilities for finding fulfillment in your profession or career. Unless you are willing to move forward with a sense of confidence and belief in yourself, you are severely limiting your access to new doors of opportunity that are waiting for you!

Embrace a Holistic Definition and Approach to Success

CORE AREA 7
A Clear Sense of Life Purpose

We all are born with unique talents and gifts. But sometimes our talents and gifts lie dormant and unused. Whether it's because we don't feel supported or because we've neglected our dreams in order to put food on the table - or any one of a number of other reasons, we arrive at a point when we know we have deviated from our true calling in life.

If you have not yet discovered your life purpose, your initial challenge is to muster the courage to find it. A clear sense of life purpose can and will be revealed to you when you are committed to finding it. Finding your unique sense of purpose begins with gaining a perspective of life that's more about giving than receiving. The more you trust in your gifts and believe that you are called to do something that is much bigger than you, the more doors will automatically open for you, leading you to fulfill your life purpose.

Below is a list of questions you can ask yourself that may serve as an excellent starting point in the process of gaining a clear sense of your unique life purpose:

1. In what ways am I passionate about helping others?
2. What do I feel or believe are my greatest gifts, talents and abilities?
3. What job, skill or talent do I possess that I enjoy and receive enough fulfillment from that I would share for free and spend hours a day doing?
4. What would be my dream job?
5. If time and money were not an obstacle, what major social cause would I want to address and how would I help people in need?
6. What do I feel I am called to do?
7. What unique talents, skills, and abilities do I possess that can be used to make the world a better place?

It is my belief that, riding above all specific jobs, professions and occupations, there is a universal life purpose and ultimate life goal that is shared by and applies to all human beings:

> The highest purpose in life
> is to learn to live a life
> of Love,
> Balance,
> Harmony,
> and Shared Abundance.

Everything else is secondary.

Anthony Parnell

I AM...SUCCESS

Chapter 3

Develop and Implement an Efficient Plan of Action

"The Words of a Philosopher……"

Is he a philosopher?
or, is he a man
who has studied
the science of life
and stories of success
and failure?

Has he studied
stories of the materialization
of unlimited potential
and stories of limited expectations
of life
and of oneself?

Has he studied
The pursuit of love,
The pursuit of wealth,
The pursuit of fame?

Yes, he has,
and the philosopher says:
What we really want –
our most intense desires…
resides at the core of our thoughts
and our beliefs about ourselves
and about the possibilities of life itself.

Develop and Implement an Efficient Plan of Action

The philosopher says:
that life truly is a canvas
upon which we paint the unfolding
of yesterday,
today,
and tomorrow's reality.

The philosopher says:
that in the pursuit and attainment
of any goal,
there are consequences and sacrifices–
known and unknown–
that must be made
in pursuit of that particular goal.

that the ability to attain one's goals
and to create the life one wants
is dependent upon the combination
of three things:

✦ Knowing, with tremendous clarity,
what it is that you want.

✦ Believing, with all of your heart and mind,
that you "will have" what you want.

✦ An openness to move into the unknown
in search of the path
that will lead you to the manifestation.......

I AM...SUCCESS

of your vision
and
intense desire.

A poem by *Anthony Parnell*
Inspired by a Philosopher

There is a dream and a vision inside of everyone. For some, it becomes crystal clear and firmly etched in their psyche during childhood. For others, it requires a journey of many years, through varied life experiences, and deep soul searching.

Some find the courage to pursue their dreams and visions. Others are too afraid to ever attempt to try because of fear of failure, disappointment or lack of faith. Nevertheless, we all are either moving towards the fulfillment of our dreams and visions or moving towards greater disappointment and limited fulfillment with life and with ourselves. No one is standing still!

By now, I hope you can see my intention: I designed this book not only to help you become crystal clear about what it is that you want to create and manifest in your life, but also to empower you to identify all the obstacles that may be impeding the level of fulfillment you are experiencing in your life.

In Chapters 1 and 2, you were provided with a *holistic* view of success that encompasses Seven Core Areas of Life Balance. Having introduced you to a philosophy and definition of success that is multi-dimensional, it now is time to begin thinking through your goals in each of the Seven Core Areas of Life Balance and defining your unique life vision.

Before actually writing out your goals, it is important to take "Personal Inventory" and assess where you are as it pertains to a *holistic* approach to success. More specifically, I would like for you to assess your strengths and weaknesses in each of the Seven Core Areas.

STOP!

Please take a few moments to think through each of your Seven Core Areas of Life Balance by completing the "Life Balance Report Card" on the following page. Give yourself a grade in each of the Seven Core Areas (A = highest level of health; F = lowest level of health).

A = Excellent

B = Good

C = Fair

D = Poor

F = Very Poor

Remember, there are no right or wrong answers. This is simply a measuring stick of how you currently view balance, harmony, and clarity of your goals in each area of your life. You may find it helpful to refer back to Chapters 1 and 2.

Once you complete the Life Balance Report Card, feel free to record any general observations of where you currently are in your life. Space for writing is provided on the page following the Report Card (page 40).

LIFE BALANCE REPORT CARD
(Self-Grade)

SEVEN CORE AREAS OF LIFE BALANCE	GRADE
Healthy Mind	
Healthy Body	
Healthy Spirit	
Healthy Finances	
Healthy Relationships	
Healthy Profession / Career	
A Clear Sense of Life Purpose	

I AM...SUCCESS

GOAL STATEMENTS and PLAN for ACHIEVING EACH GOAL

Now that you have completed the Life Balance Report Card, it is much easier to pinpoint which target areas you want to prioritize and give the greatest amount of attention. On the following pages, carefully think through specific "Goal Statements" for each of your Seven Core Areas of Life Balance. This should immediately be followed by writing the steps that you plan to take to accomplish each goal (along with setting target dates for accomplishing each milestone).

What are your current Goals and Objectives related to the Seven Core Areas of Life Balance?

I. **HEALTHY MIND**

Primary Goals:

_____

_____

_____

_____

Plan or Strategy for Achieving this specific Goal:

_____

_____

_____

_____

_____

II. **HEALTHY BODY**

Primary Goals:

_____

_____

_____

_____

Plan or Strategy for Achieving this specific Goal:

_____

_____

_____

_____

I AM...SUCCESS

III. **HEALTHY SPIRIT**

Primary Goals:

_____

_____

_____

_____

Plan or Strategy for Achieving this specific Goal:

_____

_____

_____

_____

_____

IV. **HEALTHY FINANCES**

Primary Goals:

_____

_____

_____

_____

_____

Plan or Strategy for Achieving this specific Goal:

_____

_____

_____

_____

_____

V. **HEALTHY RELATIONSHIPS**

Primary Goals:

_____

_____

_____

_____

Plan or Strategy for Achieving this specific Goal:

_____

_____

_____

_____

_____

VI. HEALTHY PROFESSION/CAREER

Primary Goals:

_____

_____

_____

_____

_____

Plan or Strategy for Achieving this specific Goal:

_____

_____

_____

_____

_____

I AM...SUCCESS

VII. A CLEAR SENSE OF LIFE PURPOSE

Primary Goals:

_____

_____

_____

_____

Plan or Strategy for Achieving this specific Goal:

_____

_____

_____

_____

PRIORITIZE WHICH GOALS ARE MOST IMPORTANT FOR YOU TO ACCOMPLISH

Now, having written clear Goal Statements for each of the Seven Core Areas and a plan for accomplishing each goal, you can prioritize them. Go back to each Core Area and list the goals according to which is most important for you to begin working on.

GOAL #1

_____

_____

_____

_____

_____

I AM...SUCCESS

GOAL #2

_____

_____

_____

_____

GOAL #3

_____

_____

_____

_____

Develop and Implement an Efficient Plan of Action

GOAL #4

_____

_____

_____

_____

_____

GOAL #5

_____

_____

_____

_____

_____

GOAL #6

_____

_____

_____

_____

GOAL #7

_____

_____

_____

_____

TAKE SMALL STEPS

Now that you have clearly defined and prioritized your goals for each of the core areas of your life, it is time to begin the work of actually implementing them. However, to ensure that you start off on the right foot, my recommendation is that you initially focus on only one goal. This will allow you to build your confidence to achieve small milestones and see tangible results from your efforts in a short period of time.

In other words, don't put too much pressure on yourself by trying to tackle too many goals at once. The initial focus should simply be on moving forward, making progress. This, generally, is best accomplished by starting with one primary goal and then breaking it down into smaller steps with target dates for achieving each milestone.

For example, you may want to get into better shape by losing ten pounds and developing a more toned physique. Dieting, then, as well as physical fitness would be key components to your broader goal of losing weight. Below is an illustration of how you can break down your target physical goals into smaller steps and create obtainable milestones.

I AM...SUCCESS

SAMPLE STEP-BY-STEP GOALS
RECREATION/EXERCISE

TODAY

I will jump rope for one minute.

THIS WEEK

I will jump rope for one minute every other day.

THIS MONTH

Week 2 — I will jump rope for two minutes every other day.

Week 3 — I will jump rope for two minutes and do fifty push-ups every   other day.

Week 4 — I will jump rope for two minutes and do fifty push-ups every other day.

3 MONTHS

I will jump rope for five minutes and do one hundred push-ups every other day.

6 MONTHS

I will jump rope for eight minutes and do 150 push-ups every other day.

1 YEAR

I will jump rope for ten minutes and do 200 push-ups every other day.

The example on the previous page is what I refer to as Step-by-Step Goals because the emphasis of the exercise is on creating an outline of how you will accomplish your self-identified goals "step-by-step" within given timelines. The greatest benefit is that you are able to focus on taking small steps in accomplishing your long-term goals as opposed to placing too much emphasis on accomplishing your ultimate goal all at once. By implementing Step-by-Step Goals, you are forced to take small steps and to be patient with the process, focusing on your growth and development one day at a time.

A second benefit is that, by establishing increments, you are more inclined to set realistic goals because you can view what is required to achieve your long-term goals more objectively. Also, Step-by-Step Goals are completely flexible according to your needs: you are able to change the timelines to ensure that your goals are based upon realistic expectations.

A final benefit is that you can feel a sense of accomplishment in a much shorter period of time as you complete some of the smaller steps required to accomplish your larger goals. Utilizing this approach might make the difference in whether or not you follow-through and maintain the long-term discipline required to accomplish your goals. For most people, receiving frequent rewards is essential for maintaining high levels of motivation.

I AM...SUCCESS

Chapter 4

Trust in Your Power to Manifest Your Life Vision: Trust in the Manifestation

*"You are a Creator.
You were born with the ability
to create the life you want."*

Anthony Parnell

See Yourself as a Creator

Over the past decade, the notion of "The Law of Attraction" has become increasingly popular among people from all walks of life. It surely seems to have found a secure place within the American vernacular of the 21st century. Yet, even while proving to be a life-changing concept for millions of people, I believe that we can take this concept a step further.

What if you stopped seeing yourself simply as a person who **attracts** prosperity, success, and the like?

Instead, what if you begin to also see yourself as a **creator** of prosperity and success?

Wow, let's think for a moment about the difference between **Attracting** something vs. **Creating** something!!

Understanding the contrast between these two actions can mean a world of difference in someone's life! It certainly did in mine. One day a light bulb went off in my head. I suddenly realized that I should not be satisfied with seeing myself only as an "Attractor" and that it was important to know I am also a "Creator"! To me, being a "Creator" means to exercise my ability to access a much greater sense of personal power.

A "Creator" is someone who becomes an ongoing, continuous life force whose magnetism not only "attracts" things to it but also gives birth to new life. One aspect of being a "creator" is when we are intentional in using our creative energy, therefore making specific decisions and choices in order to make something happen. A second aspect of being a "creator" is the unconscious and subsconscious things that automatically happen or occur in our lives because of the vibrations that we are emitting at that particular point/moment in our life.

It is my belief that all human beings are built for success which means that we are built to be creators. We are not built for failure. The difference is whether or not our natural makeup has been nurtured and reinforced or if we have been reprogrammed for failure.

This book is entitled "I AM…SUCCESS" because it affirms a belief and an approach to life that recognizes our abilities to create, attract, and manifest what we desire as inherent traits. In other words, the ability to attract and the ability to create are God-given attributes that are implanted in all individuals at birth. You simply have to tap into these abilities and hone your skills for creating your goals and life vision.

As human beings, we radiate both positive and negative energies that are reflected in our thoughts and actions. As a result, within the context of our current emotional, mental, physical, and spiritual states, we possess the ability to attract positive and negative life events (whether consciously or unconsciously). The more we see ourselves as both attractors and creators, the more we can focus our energies and efforts toward bringing what we desire into our lives.

Life is filled with challenges and adversity. Some are easy to overcome, and some take a tremendous toll on us emotionally, mentally and physically. When you are faced with a daunting challenge that leaves you feeling frustrated and defeated, what primary tool/s do you rely upon? What do you keep in your tool kit for digging yourself out of an emotional rut?

I believe the most basic tool is simply a promise to yourself that you will remain totally committed to confront any and all obstacles that you know are keeping you from achieving your goals.

The Primary Rule: Focus Attention On What You Want – not what you don't want!

Time and time again, in my own life and in the lives of others, I've seen the attitude adjustment as expressed in The Primary Rule completely alter an individual's state of being; namely, from feeling frustrated and helpless to feeling optimistic and motivated. The simple truth is that we often focus all of our energy on getting rid of what we don't want, namely, the obstacles, instead of "keeping our eyes on the prize" and focusing on what it is that we want! Just by making this one shift, you can automatically change your mental and emotional state from negative to positive. This is not ignoring the reality of any frustrating situations or circumstances that may be staring you in the face such as excessive debt, serious marital problems, social or academic challenges in school or extended unemployment. Instead, it is adopting a personal philosophy or life principle that enables you to speak, feel, and think with positive energy. The more you apply this philosophy in your daily life, the more likely it is that you will observe an increase of positive events unfolding in your life.

By <u>Focusing Attention More On What You Want,</u> you greatly increase the probability of attracting the desires of your heart.

This is because you automatically trigger from within a creative energy that inspires you to develop a plan for fulfilling your goal. Even better, you may become such a powerful magnetic life force that you will attract what you desire in ways you never imagined!

The power of positive thinking when followed by positive actions has been proven to be effective by many people in all walks of life. Here, however, my intention is not to debate the scientific validity of the power of the law of attraction and the power of positive thinking. I simply want to introduce you to a different way of approaching obstacles when you encounter them. If the strategy you have been using works for you, then all the more power to you. But, if you're not getting the results you want in your life (with your relationships, career, finances, and so on), the place I strongly urge you to start is by closely examining your mental attitude and your mental focus. ***If your mind is not filled with thoughts of success and accomplishing your goals, then, you are stifling your ability to fully activate your personal power.***

When clients, family and friends reach out to me for advice, insight and emotional support, one of the primary things I assess is their mental attitude. To this end, I will ask several key questions very directly: "Where are you focusing your attention? Are you directing your attention within yourself (internally) or outside yourself (externally)? Is your mind overwhelmed with thoughts about the problem? Or, is your mind working creatively with thoughts about the solution to your problem? Are you able to clearly visualize in your mind how the problem can be resolved?"

Let me share with you a great example of the power of **Focusing Attention More On What You Want – not what you don't want.**

Several months ago, I received a call from a client who was in the process of starting a business at the young age of 20. This young lady was living at home and going to school full-time while working a full-time job. Despite having so much on her plate at such an early age, she was determined to move out and find her own place. I had strongly advised against it considering the low rent she was paying by living at home, the amount of stress she was feeling from trying to keep up with her current bills, and the unpredictability of revenue and cash flow that typically comes with starting a new business. I was particularly concerned about how she would hold up physically and emotionally if another financial responsibility was added to her already overwhelming debt load.

I clearly remember the day she frantically called me expressing how frustrated she was with her current living arrangement. She argued that it had become too unbearable. So, she decided to pack up her things and move out immediately.

This was actually the fifth call over a two to three-week period in which she emphatically declared that she was fed up with living at home. For some reason, this time she said something that caused me to view her situation a little differently. Despite the limited money she had for moving, I, too, began to feel her situation was becoming too detrimental for her to continue living there.

Throughout our conversations, I kept hoping to hear her say that she was developing some kind of plan for moving; maybe putting aside a certain amount of money each month or talking to friends or relatives about finding a place - just the basic steps that anyone would need to think about if they really want to make a move.

Instead, the only thing I continually heard – always wrapped in lots of emotion! – was how awful and unbearable her living conditions were and how she resented living with her parents.

That's when I carefully explained to her that the primary reason she's currently feeling helpless and powerless is because she was focusing all her attention on what she doesn't want in her life (her current living situation) as opposed to focusing on what she does want (a new living situation)!

As she was processing and digesting what I had conveyed to her, I asked her, "Can you tell me some things you could do right now to prepare to move if you made a conscious choice to focus your emotional, mental and physical attention and energy on what you want?"

Within a few seconds, she said, "Start looking for a new place to live…..but, I don't have enough money to move."

I quickly replied, "Okay, you're off to a great start! But that's just one example. I'm talking about creating a very detailed list of every possible thing you can do that exemplifies focusing more attention on what you do want in terms of a better place to live as opposed to spending the majority of your day thinking about why you hate your current living situation."

I added, "Everyone who has a goal doesn't always start out with all the money they need to accomplish their goal."

There is a thing called "faith." When you have "faith" and become disciplined in focusing more of your thoughts and attention on what you want rather than what you don't want, very often, the money you need appears in a variety of forms. But, first, you must believe that your mental attitude and your faith, *together*, create a power that can help you effect this type of change in your life.

To further illustrate my point, I asked her, "How much better do you think you would feel if you got in your car right now and drove around to several places and posted flyers that read:

College Student Seeks Room for Rent

You definitely would feel better because you would feel empowered as opposed to feeling helpless. And, that's why you need to hang up the phone right now and start writing or typing a detailed list of all the things **you will do** starting today to ensure that you're focusing more of your attention on what you want rather than what you don't want. Then, as soon as you finish, send the list to me in a text message."

She agreed, and about ten minutes later, I received a text message from her with a detailed list. After reviewing it, I made a few minor adjustments. Here is the final draft:

1. **Create a Flyer that reads:**
   "College Student Seeks Room for Rent"

2. **Pass out Flyer to College Classmates**

3. **Post Flyer at local colleges**

4. **Post Flyer at Laundromats**

5. **Post Ad on Craigslist**

6. **Search Roommate Ads on Craigslist**

7. **Write out an Affirmation Statement of what I want**

8. **Recite my Affirmation several times a day, as needed**

The icing on the cake came for her when I wrote out an "affirmation" statement that summarized with total clarity exactly what she wanted. The strategy was for her to read the affirmation and recite it out loud as many times a day as necessary in order for her to maintain a positive mental attitude. This is the affirmation I created for her:

> *"I am making forward progress in my life. What appears to be obstacles are only temporary delays. I am mentally, emotionally, and financially prepared to move, and because I am 100% ready to move, I am creating doors of opportunity for a wonderful new residence to appear in my life (to manifest itself), easily and effortlessly, that is affordable and conveniently located in close proximity to my school and my work."*

As a Life Coach and Business Coach, there are many strategies and approaches that I utilize in trying to help my clients, family, and friends move forward when they're feeling stuck and/or trying to gain clarity in a specific situation. The example I just shared with you represents, in a nutshell, some of the most fundamental elements that must be present for any individual who has a specific goal they are working toward—whether it be personal or professional.

SUMMARY

First, a person needs to be completely clear about what exactly it is they desire or want to accomplish. A good indicator of sufficient clarity is being able to articulate what the specific goal or desire is.

Secondly, a person needs a clear plan or strategy for how they're going to achieve the goal AND the discipline to persist and follow through with the plan.

Thirdly, a person needs to be able to maintain a positive mental attitude even when they are faced with major challenges and obstacles to the plan.

I believe Focusing Attention On What You Want is not only one of the strongest but one of the most simplistic approaches that you can use as a starting point for accomplishing your goals. Of course, there are many other ingredients and variables that can come into play such as "The Power of Faith" and "The Power of Visual Imagery." These are discussed next. Please continue!

Exercise the Power of Faith

I came to a point in my life when I began to wrestle with the meaning of "faith." What is faith? Can I develop it? If so, *how* do I develop it?

These questions about faith are very significant for me given my strong religious background. I labored for many years sorting through what I believed to be misinterpretations and miseducation surrounding the true meaning and practice of faith.

Fortunately, I found my way out of the maze. I found a definition of faith that I feel is not only clear but concise. And, it does not impose any limitations as I continue to pursue my goals.

I have come to define "faith" in this way:

> *"An unwavering belief that one's prayer has already been answered."*

This means I have a consistent thought pattern telling me that my goals and desires will eventually manifest themselves. There is a sense of expectancy and belief that it is just a matter of time before my desires will materialize.

It also means that I am not easily overcome with doubt when challenges and obstacles arise. I don't go into a panicked state of thinking, and I don't get off course with my plan of action.

When I have faith, feelings of frustration and disappointment are only temporary. Even if I decide to reassess the approach I'm using to accomplish my goals, and make a determination that a different, better strategy should be employed, there remains a strong and enduring sense of belief that I will eventually get there. This is the "Power of Faith." It sees the invisible and believes that what has not yet materialized *will* materialize!

Utilize the Power of Visual Imagery

Visual Imagery is basically using your imagination to see your goal or desire coming to fruition.

Visual Imagery is at work all the time in our everyday lives even when we're not consciously thinking of it. It's at play among professional athletes the night before a major sporting event such as football, basketball or boxing.

For example, what if you were to go into a team's locker room at the Super Bowl right before the game? You would immediately feel the intensity and see deep concentration in their faces. Upon witnessing this, you would probably be convinced that each player is free from any doubt about winning. Indeed, if you asked any one of them directly, he would most certainly say that they will be taking home the trophy!

Why do they have such a strong sense of belief?

I can tell you that it's not just because they've worked hard to put themselves in this position – which indeed they have.

And it's not just because they have an intense passion for their profession and a desire to be champions – which indeed they do.

Much of it is because they have developed a heightened sense of visual imagery.

Over and over in their minds, they have envisioned themselves as the winners…holding up the championship trophy…celebrating with their families and friends.

Even if deep down inside they really don't believe they're better than their opponent, they know that, in the final days before the event, it is not only their physical preparation that counts but also their mental preparation; they must get into a zone, or mental state, of intense concentration and visualization.

They know that they must go into the game believing they can win. They know that when competing at the highest level against other professional athletes, physical ability alone is not enough to guarantee a win. They must also have the right mental attitude.

In addition to developing a strategy, a big part of their mental preparation is telling themselves, "As long as we believe we can win, then, even if we're outmatched or not performing our best, we still have a great chance of winning!"

Mental preparation is the game changer (literally!) in countless major sporting events. We've seen it time and time again when the so-called "best team" does not win. Very often, the team – or in a sport like boxing, the individual athlete – who wins is better prepared mentally. Using visual imagery helps athletes or anyone to become more focused and mentally stronger.

In American culture, there is an infatuation with the "Cinderella" story: we can't resist loving the underdog! This is the person (or team) that is greatly underestimated yet somehow comes out on top. Even though they may not be as talented, as gifted, as attractive or as popular, etc., they manage to be the winner! I believe it is due to their physical and mental toughness as well as a willingness to out-work (or out-play) their opponent; to persist in trying to gain the advantage – the winning edge - over whoever it is they find themselves up against. It's very likely that many of the individual athletes or teams who are not predicted to win draw inspiration from being considered the "underdog."

VISUAL IMAGERY EXERCISE

You don't have to be an athlete to consciously practice and utilize the power of visual imagery, that is, the power of your imagination. Mental focus, mental preparation, and visual imagery are powerful tools that are available to everyone.

EXERCISE:

First, think about one of the primary goals you have in your life. If you have it written or memorized, read or recite it out loud.

Then, get comfortably seated in a chair or on the floor. Take slow, deep breathes to relax yourself.

Close your eyes and try to completely empty your mind.

Continue with a slow and steady repetition of breathing in and breathing out until you feel your shoulders and your whole body become completely relaxed and still.

Once you find yourself completely relaxed with your mind clear of any thoughts, focus your attention on one single goal you want to achieve.

Again, slowly read or recite the primary goal you have selected to focus on.

Continue to focus by visualizing your goal. In your mind, see yourself accomplishing the goal, bringing to fruition whatever it is you are pursuing. If it's a personal fitness goal, visualize posing in the mirror and loving what you see.

Try your best to sustain the visual image of accomplishing your goal. Attempt to hold that one single thought, without allowing any other thoughts to enter your mind, for as long as you feel comfortable doing so – whether it's many seconds or many minutes.

Approach Visual Imagery not just as an intellectual experience but also as an emotional experience. Once you can clearly visualize your goal being fulfilled, connect to the emotions you anticipate feeling the moment that your goal or desire is fulfilled.
Feel the excitement! Feel the happiness! Feel the relief!

Think about your goals….

Visualize your goals being fulfilled…

Feel the emotion of your goals being fulfilled…

You may find that the hardest part of this exercise is getting completely still and quiet and emptying your mind. It may be extremely difficult to completely shut off the part of yourself that is consumed with thoughts, worries and concerns for your family, your job, your long "To-Do" list, and so on.

When trying this for the first time, keep in mind that, just like any exercise, it may take practice before you feel completely comfortable doing it. However, if over time you're still having difficulty holding on to the visualization for even 10 – 15 seconds, this may be an indication that there is too much "emotional clutter" in your life. When we allow negative stress to build up, it literally can weigh us down.

Sometimes we worry about things that are out of our control or experience mental overload from trying to process too many things at once.

In my own experiences of practicing visual imagery, I have noticed greater success with minimizing emotional clutter and blocking out distractions when I hold on to the vision of my goal for at least 10 seconds. At the 10 second mark I can feel that I'm generating enough emotional energy in the visualization. This is because the emotions connected to the fulfillment of my goal continue to well up as I maintain a clear mental image. Remember: Do not approach Visual Imagery strictly through the intellect – as a "thought experience" - but also through your emotions - as a "feeling experience."

MIND BODY PARTNERSHIP

The bottom line is that there are moments in our lives when, although we have a great desire to accomplish a specific goal, we just can't seem to get into the right mental state to do what we need to do. There are too many distractions internally and/or externally that impede our ability to create enough single-mindedness in the pursuit of our goals. Or, we don't have enough faith, will power, or resourcefulness.

I'm not speaking of a single-minded obsession where we lose all sense of a balanced approach to living life. I'm simply speaking of our ability to possess a dominant thought that is so powerful it serves as a motivation or driving force for positive change in our lives.

The truth is that single-mindedness is what enables many different kinds of people to accomplish very ambitious undertakings: graduating from college; passing the bar exam to become a lawyer; finishing medical school to become a doctor; qualifying for the Olympics.

It's unavoidable that some goals require more time, energy, and mental focus than others. When this is the case, you have to decide whether or not you're willing to invest the prerequisite amount of time and energy that is necessary to fulfill that particular goal.

Remember, the work that is required of you to fulfill your goals is not just about how hard you work physically. In most instances, the fulfillment of your goals is equally dependent upon your mental focus and mind power. The mind/body partnership is a truly remarkable collaboration that we should always be aware of as we work to accomplish our goals – both large and small!

"I AM...Success"

The moment
we think a thought
it possesses the innate potential
of taking on
a life of its own.

Whether our thoughts
are positive or negative,
they transform themselves
into Energy,
and Motion.

I AM...SUCCESS

The ability to control our thoughts,
then,
is synonymous
with the ability to control our Destiny.

Fear
is a Negative thought.
I shall not live in Fear.
I shall not live my life
allowing Negative thoughts
to consume me.
I shall not allow
thoughts of failure
to comfortably reside in my mind.
I shall not allow
thoughts of fear and failure
to be stronger in my mind
and in my spirit
than the positive thoughts of strength and success,
because the power to change my circumstances
resides within The Inner Workings of My Mind…
My Thought Patterns…
My Faith…
My Belief…
The Efficient Action that I exercise…

This is why
I AM…….
SUCCESS!!!

Anthony Parnell

Chapter 5

Fulfill Your Vision of Success: Your Life Vision

"A Mantra of Success"

We have everything
we need
to be successful
in our endeavors.

As long as we move forward
with intense passion,
persistence,
and absolute clarity of vision
and purpose,
we can attract into our lives
all the tangible and intangible resources
we need
to fulfill our goals
and our life vision.

Anthony Parnell

ARE YOU READY TO MANIFEST YOUR VISION OF SUCCESS?

Many times in life, we think we're ready to achieve a particular goal or fulfill our overall vision of success. Our confidence is high. We feel a strong sense of determination. We have an intense desire, a tireless work ethic, and a willingness to do whatever it takes to accomplish our goal.

But, for whatever reason, we just can't seem to get over the hump.

Some barriers and obstacles that we come across on our path to success are clearly visible. When we don't have enough money, or don't know the right people, or don't have the right skills, it's usually right in our face! But sometimes there are barriers stifling us that we can't see and for this reason they often cause us the greatest damage.

It's easy to tell ourselves and to believe "If only I could see these invisible barriers and obstacles that are impeding my forward progress, then I could just move them out of the way." But, that's much easier said than done. Invisible barriers – those that are not physical, material, or tangible in nature - often exist because we have not yet evolved to a place in which we can discern them. Such barriers include those that exist in our minds (our thought patterns) and the energy that we are vibrating and projecting into the world.

Our sense of personal power increases when we develop the ability to shift or transform the energy vibrations within ourselves and in our physical environment. We truly begin to tap into a higher level of personal power when we are able to remain focused on our goals, our sense of life purpose, and our overall vision of success, *even when our immediate external environment is not conducive to our success.* Working ourselves out of a non-supportive situation requires clarity of purpose, mental fortitude, a strong sense of faith and belief, and a heightened sense of self-awareness.

IDENTIFY AND REMOVE BARRIERS

In order to successfully overcome barriers – both visible and hidden, it is essential to work on building your mind power so as to create more discipline in your daily behaviors. Just as we are what we eat, so, too, are we the products of our mental habits. You must train your mind to think positively if you want positive things to happen in your life.

You must also commit yourself to developing greater self-awareness. This will enable you to consistently identify hidden barriers. Your commitment to a minimum of "5 Minutes A Day" of writing and self-reflection is critical for realigning yourself with a sustained mental focus, supported mainly by positive thoughts and positive visions of your success. This can be in the form of prayer, meditation, daily journaling, and/or reading or reciting your goal statements and affirmations.

Ultimately, it is up to you to decide whether you will employ long-term solutions to removing barriers in your life or whether you will continue going through the daily motions of life without achieving some of your most important goals.

A great place to start is by first identifying some of the internal and external barriers that are preventing you from achieving your goals. Then, begin developing and implementing prioritized strategies that are designed to address each of the barriers you have identified.

In the following table, I've listed some internal and external barriers that frequently impede or limit our ability to achieve success.

I AM...SUCCESS

Please take a few moments to closely review each list. Then, circle any of the barriers that are currently impeding or limiting your ability to achieve success.

Also, add to the list any additional internal or external barriers that you identify.

BARRIERS TO ACHIEVING YOUR GOALS	
Internal	**External**
Lack of clarity	Wrong or unsupportive circle of friends
Lack of mental focus and discipline	
	Wrong or unsupportive circle of business associates
Lack of faith and belief	
Poor or undeveloped plan for achieving your goals and attaining your vision of success	Strained relationships with family members
Undisciplined work habits/poor work habits	Unhealthy living environment
Living in the past – difficulty forgiving	Not living in the ideal city where there is a high demand for your talents and skills
Fear of failure	
Fear of poverty	
Fear of success	Lack of capital
Feelings of guilt	

I AM...SUCCESS

Now that you have examined this general list of potential barriers, please list any barriers identified that apply to you personally.

_____

_____

_____

_____

Were you able to think of any personal barriers that do not appear on the list provided? If so, write them down here:

_____

_____

_____

_____

In the following exercise, you're going to prioritize the top three barriers from your list that you would like to begin addressing immediately in your personal or professional life.

PRIORITIZE 3 BARRIERS

1) _____

_____

2) _____

_____

3) _____

_____

What strategies do you plan to utilize to address each of these barriers?

REWRITE PRIORITIZED BARRIER #1

_____

_____

_____

PLAN or STRATEGY for Addressing BARRIER #1:

_____

_____

_____

_____

_____

_____

_____

REWRITE PRIORITIZED BARRIER #2

_____

_____

_____

PLAN or STRATEGY for Addressing BARRIER #2:

_____

_____

_____

_____

_____

_____

_____

_____

_____

REWRITE PRIORITIZED BARRIER #3

_____

_____

_____

PLAN or STRATEGY for Addressing BARRIER #3:

_____

_____

_____

_____

_____

_____

_____

_____

FORGIVE YOURSELF FOR PAST FAILURES

Prosperity and Success are not created
when one's thoughts
are intensely focused
on failures and disappointments
of the past.

Prosperity and Success
is attained
when one's thoughts and actions
are intently focused
on what currently lies within one's power
and control.

Anthony Parnell

No matter how painful your past failures and disappointments have been, you can regain your composure, begin again and move forward. However, to do so you must believe in yourself 100%!

This begins with forgiving yourself and others for your past failures and shortcomings.

You must be at peace with yourself knowing that you did everything within your power at that time to produce the desired outcome. And, if there's a reason to think that you didn't do everything that you could have done, you must now tell yourself repeatedly that "Today is a new day! I have moved beyond the past. I am a new person!"

In time, you will regain your self-confidence and restore a belief in yourself and in life!

If you're continuing to feel stuck in this area and unable to forgive yourself for past failures-even after trying to maintain a positive attitude, here is a simple exercise that you can do to work through your unresolved emotions:

Make A List of Your Greatest Disappointments

EXERCISE

Make a list of Your Greatest Disappointments

- *In the last six months*

  _____
  _____
  _____

- *In the last year*

  _____
  _____
  _____

- *In your lifetime*

  _____
  _____
  _____

Ask Yourself:

- *"What internal or external resources or skills were lacking at that time of my life?"*

  _____
  _____
  _____
  _____
  _____
  _____

-

- *What could I have done differently?*

  _____
  _____
  _____

- *How have I committed myself to strengthening any areas of weakness and identifying and/or developing the resources I lacked?*

  _____
  _____
  _____

- *Once I've gained or regained enough self-confidence, what will be the primary goal that is most important for me to pursue?*

  _____
  _____
  _____

- *What healthy forms of support and accountability will I utilize this time to help me accomplish my goal while maintaining emotional equilibrium?*

  _____
  _____
  _____

- *What specific plan will I implement in pursuit of this goal:*

  - *In the next 24 hours*
    _____
    _____

  - *In the next week*
    _____
    _____

  - *In the next month*
    _____
    _____

  - *In the next 3 months*
    _____
    _____

  - *In the next 6 months*
    _____
    _____

  - *In the next year*
    _____
    _____
    _____
    _____

FIVE MINUTES A DAY OF WRITING & SELF-REFLECTION

Our long-term goals are not achieved overnight. Especially if you're dreaming big, it generally takes time to manifest your goals and desires. Therefore, just as you should have a plan for accomplishing your goals, you should also have a plan for maintaining balance and not letting your intense focus on accomplishing your goals negatively affect your physical, emotional, and mental health. It's important that you don't "burnout" in the pursuit of your goals.

One way to avoid burnout is to build in a regular routine of extracurricular activities. Involvement in a mixture of various healthy actions will allow you to release the build-up of negative emotions and any negative energy. For example, two outlets I use consistently are playing basketball and watching great documentary films *(see The Seven Laws of Stress Management, Anthony Parnell, 2018. Published by Books By Anthony Parnell)*.

Secondly, you must implement a regular routine of being still or quiet. As discussed on page 81, I recommend "5 Minutes A Day" for writing and self-reflection. Self-reflection can be in the form of prayer, meditation, visualization, or whatever you discover that suits you best. When journaling, the "5 Minutes A Day" should be a free-flowing experience in which you record any thoughts and emotions that come into your consciousness. In both your journaling/writing and self-reflection, it is always good to periodically revisit your goal statements and affirm your intended purpose.

Do not be overly concerned whether you are using correct grammar when writing down your ideas. The emphasis should solely be placed on fully expressing your thoughts and emotions.

Six Steps to Picking Up the Pen

If you experience difficulty getting started or maintaining a consistent flow with writing, here are "Six Steps to Picking Up the Pen" that you can use to get in the flow. These steps are taken from my book *Healing Through Writing: A Journaling Guide to Emotional and Spiritual Growth*. If used properly, these steps should greatly aid you in your ability to relax and focus on writing.

1. Set A Time

>Select a time of day that is best for you to concentrate and focus your energy (morning, afternoon, after dinner, before bed, and so on). This is a time that you feel would be most conducive for you to write. My mind is most clear early in the morning or late at night. Whatever time you choose, make sure you take a moment or two to unwind and transition from your previous activity. For instance, instead of trying to immediately write, take a few moments to pause and reflect on any recent progress you've made. This may prove beneficial in creating a sense of organization to your thoughts and emotions.

2. Choose a Comfortable Location to Write

>Think of a relaxing environment in which you are not likely to be interrupted or distracted. Also, consider a location in your

home or office where you feel the greatest sense of peace or positive energy.

3. Set The Mood with Music

Once you have set a time and located a comfortable, relaxing environment, you will have to determine whether a certain style of music will be required to set the mood. It is important that both your mind and body are calm and relaxed, enabling you to channel your energy and focus on your inner self. For most beginners, music will be necessary to help them sustain their focus. Even after years of practice and experience, there still are times when it is extremely difficult for me to identify or express my intense emotions without the aid of some music that resonates with my mood. The right music setting the right mood helps me to relax and become more open to my thoughts and emotions. With practice and time, you too will be able to identify the source of your emotions and freely express them.

4. Focus On Breathing

Sit with your legs folded, close your eyes, and take long, slow, deep breaths to relax your body and clear your mind. As you breathe, inhale through your nose and exhale through your mouth. When inhaling, focus on taking in positive energy and filling your lungs and chest with air. While slowly exhaling, focus on releasing negative energy. Be careful of the pace of your breathing so as to not become dizzy. Then ask yourself, "How do I feel?" as you continue taking long, slow deep breaths and gradually become content with silence and stillness.

Even if no thoughts come to mind, there is therapeutic value in sitting in silence with your mind and body completely relaxed. Even though you have closed your eyes, begin writing as soon as you become conscious of the thoughts that enter your mind or as you begin to feel emotions surfacing. Be patient with the process, and if you lose your thoughts, simply refocus on the music.

Also, remind yourself that this is a process that takes time, especially if there are years of underlying emotion that have not been fully acknowledged or identified.

5. Write Your Real Emotions

Release expectations of others and the urge to judge your emotions. In learning to accept your emotions, you are learning to accept yourself where you are in your process of spiritual growth and self-awareness.

6. Take Small Steps

On a daily basis, celebrate each accomplishment. Congratulate yourself for having the discipline to write, even if only for five minutes.

Focus on consistency and detail. Remember: With time and practice you will develop the ability to honestly and succinctly express your thoughts and emotions through the healthy medium of writing.

MINIMIZE THE AMOUNT OF TIME YOU SPEND AROUND PEOPLE WHO HABITUALLY EXERCISE NEGATIVE THINKING AND NEGATIVE BEHAVIOR

The people we interact with on a daily basis are either giving us energy or taking energy from us. Thus, in the pursuit of our life goals, one of the biggest responsibilities we must shoulder is maintaining a heightened sense of awareness of our current needs emotionally and spiritually and whether or not the individuals we interact with regularly are giving us energy. The more time we spend with individuals who habitually exercise negative thinking and negative behavior, the more difficult it is for us to maintain a sense of balance and stay focused on our goals.

Living our lives in total isolation, however, is not the answer. The reality is that we all experience moments when we need a solid support system to call upon and lean on. Therefore, it is critically important to ensure that we have an adequate support system around us to help us navigate the challenges we will face in pursuit of our life goals. In addition to trying our best to maintain healthy, loving and fulfilling relationships with our families and friends currently in our lives, it is also important that we do not limit ourselves. We must be proactive in our efforts to expand our support system, both personally and professionally. To this end, we should actively seek out appropriate mentors, prayer partners and/or social groups that we can join or create – people with whom the exchange of energy is mutual and reciprocal.

MAINTAIN A CLEAR VISION : FINE-TUNE AND FOLLOW THROUGH WITH YOUR PLAN

Many individuals lose their vision of success or fail to achieve their goals because they lack discipline. They fail to follow-through with their plan.

Or, there is nothing to follow-through on because they never take the time to fully develop a clear plan or strategy in the first place.

I hope this isn't you! I hope you are not squandering the potential that you have to be happy and fulfilled.

If it is, then I want to remind you that it's never too late to renew your efforts to be happy and fulfilled. If you're willing to make the commitment to pursue your goals and your life vision of *holistic* success, there are many resources at your disposal.

This book, for one, provides a solid launch pad for you to jumpstart a new approach to accomplishing your life goals and being your best self. Use it to gain clarity, to develop a solid plan, and to begin moving forward.

As you progress from day to day, don't be reluctant to fine-tune and make adjustments to your plan as needed. It's not uncommon, even for individuals who are fully committed and well on their way to accomplishing their goals, to tweak the plan they started with. This actually should be expected and embraced as part of the process of figuring out what works and what doesn't work.

From my own experience, I am proud to say that making wise adjustments to your original strategy is an area where mentors can be especially helpful. A mentor can offer tremendous insight and excellent feedback as it pertains to your plan or strategy. I have personally witnessed how the insight of an experienced mentor has saved people weeks, months or even years of wasted time and energy.

CELEBRATE YOUR SUCCESS!!!

Sometimes, there are moments in life when we feel unstoppable; that we cannot fail; that we have discovered our true passion in life and know how to focus on our strengths; that we have learned to maximize the utilization of our gifts, talents, and abilities; and that we have surrounded ourselves with like-minded and like-spirited individuals who share our same values in life, personally and professionally.

This is when we know life is good! Life is great! We are reaping what we have sown. The seeds of success that were planted long ago have finally taken root and have begun to blossom!

Hopefully, this book will not only give you a practical tool to help you achieve the success you want but also serve as a reminder to celebrate your successes along the way. Take time to reflect on how far you have come and the lessons you have learned. Record these milestones in a "prayers answered" journal, a photo album, or something similar, and share life's precious moments with those who have provided you with unconditional love and unwavering support.

Equally important, strive to live each day by this philosophy:

> The highest purpose in life
> is to learn to live a life
> of Love,
> Balance,
> Harmony,
> and Shared Abundance.
>
> Everything else is secondary.
>
> Anthony Parnell

ABOUT THE AUTHOR

Anthony Parnell, M.S.W. is a Life Coach, Business Coach, and published author of several books. He also hosts the Podcast "The Anthony Parnell Show" where he interviews a wide range of guests discussing topics related to achieving your personal and professional goals while attaining a *holistic* definition of success. To learn more about the products and services of the Anthony Parnell brand, visit **www.AnthonyParnell.com**.

"Begin Achieving Your Life Goals Now!"

Do you or someone you know have something you want to change or achieve in your life? Maybe you'd like to...

- Start or Grow a Business
- Find new Love or Improve Your Relationships
- Get a New Career (or a raise)
- Gain a Clear Sense of Direction (Prioritize Your Goals)
- Utilize Support and Accountability in following through with Your Goals
- Find a Sense of Balance and Organization in Managing your Busy Schedule

SCHEDULE a "FREE" 30-minute "RAPID CHANGE" Coaching Session

We'll work together to...

- Create a crystal-clear vision for "holistic success" so you know exactly what you want, where you're headed, and what you need to do to make it happen.
- Uncover hidden challenges that may be sabotaging your ability to make changes that last or that are slowing down your progress in achieving your goals.
- Help re-energize and inspire you to finally achieve the change you seek - once and for all.

Email Anthony at anthony@anthonyparnell.com
Visit www.AnthonyParnell.com

www.AnthonyParnell.com

Sources of Inspiration

Byrne, Rhonda. The Secret. Simon & Schuster, 2006.

Dyer, Wayne. (1989). You'll See It When You Believe It: The Way to Your Personal Transformation. Harper Collins, 1989.

Gawain, Shakti. Creative Visualization: Use the Power of Your Imagination to Create What You Want in Your Life. Nataraj Publishing, 2002.

Gladwell, Malcolm. Outliers: The Story of Success. Little, Brown & Company, 2011.

Hill, Napoleon. Think and Grow Rich. The Penguin Group, 2005.

Kiyosaki, Robert. Rich Dad, Poor Dad. Plata Publishing, 1997.

Murphy, Joseph. The Power of Your Subconscious Mind. Bantam Books, 2000.

Orman, Suze. The Laws of Money. Free Press, 2003.

Orman, Suze. The Courage to be Rich. The Berkley Publishing Group, 2001.

Redfield, James. The Celestine Prophecy. Grand Central Publishing, 2006.

www.ingramcontent.com/pod-product-compliance
Lightning Source LLC
Chambersburg PA
CBHW050841160426
43192CB00011B/2118